How Plants Grow and Change

by Jane St. John

Plant Features

All plants are made of small building blocks called cells. Because of this, a giant oak tree is far more similar to a daffodil than you might think. Plants have many kinds of cells in common. Cells make up tissues, and tissues make up organs. Different parts of plants help water, sunlight, and other material be turned into food for the plant.

Plants need sunlight and water in order to live and grow. Plants also need carbon dioxide from the air and minerals from the soil.

Many of a daffodil's cells are similar to the cells of an oak tree.

Photosynthesis

Unlike animals, plants are able to make their own food in the form of sugar. The process plants go through to make food is called **photosynthesis.** A plant's leaves absorb carbon dioxide from the air. Its roots absorb water from the soil. Photosynthesis occurs when the plant uses sunlight and water to change carbon dioxide into food.

Oxygen and water, the waste products of photosynthesis, move into the air through tiny openings on the leaves. The stem carries food to other parts of the plant where it can be stored.

Chloroplasts

Photosynthesis takes place in the parts of leaves called chloroplasts. Chloroplasts are made up of **chlorophyll.** This is the material that gives plants their green color. Chlorophyll also takes energy from the Sun and turns water, carbon dioxide, and minerals into sugars, oxygen, and other foods.

This potato has received very little sunlight and is pale in color.

This potato has received lots of sunlight and is growing well.

Plant Parts

Most plants are made of many millions of cells. Cells can do similar jobs in every plant. Cells that do the same kind of job are put into the same group. For example, some cells help carry water or minerals through a plant. Similar cells group together to form a tissue. Bark is an example of this. Other groups of cells also work together as tissues. These tissues form organs, which keep the plant alive. A plant's organs include its leaves, stems, and roots. You will find most of these parts in plants no matter what their size or appearance, from daffodils to oak trees.

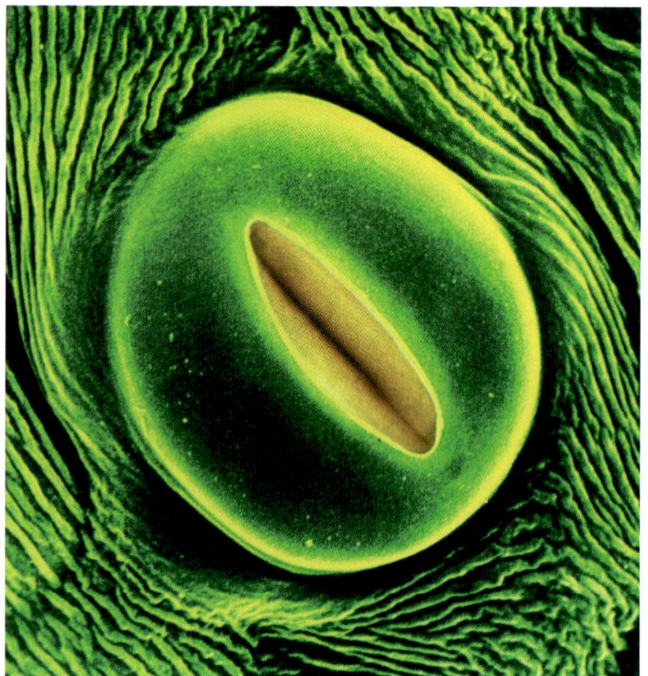

This special plant cell lets air in and out of the leaf.

Leaves

All leaves have the same job, no matter what plant they belong to. Their role is to make food so that the plant can live. Leaves come in particular forms and shapes that make it easier for the plant to make food. For example, the leaves of the cactus are needles. Their shape prevents the plant from losing water in a desert environment, where it rarely rains. Other plants, such as the palm, grow in rain forests or other places with lots of shade and rainfall. Their leaves are very wide. It is important in an ecosystem such as a rain forest that leaves be large in order to absorb as much sunlight as possible. Unlike desert plants, rain forest plants have to work harder to gain access to the sunlight they need to survive.

umbrella tree leaf

Cactus needles are leaves.

Stems

What does the thick trunk of a tree have in common with a flower? They are both stems. Even though stems range in size from thick to thin, they have the same two main functions. First, they carry water and food between the roots of a plant and its leaves. Second, they physically prop up, or support, the plant. They help hold the leaves up so they can get as much sunlight as they need.

Some stems are very easy to bend. You probably know that the stems of common flowers or plants in your garden—lilies, tulips, and peas, for example—are soft. These stems are normally green and help the plant carry out photosynthesis, as do the leaves. Other stems, such as the trunks of trees, are thick and strong. The outside layer of cells on a tree is dead. It forms a material called bark that helps to protect the tree from damage.

Roots

Have you ever been helping with garden work and had to pull out weeds? Many weeds give a good example of what roots do. Roots help keep a plant in the ground. A plant's roots are mostly underground, so they can constantly take in water and minerals from the soil. They grow and get strong in this way.

Roots, however, cannot make food, since root cells don't contain chlorophyll. Some roots, however, can store food. A plant can use this stored food if it cannot make enough food during the process of photosynthesis.

This root vegetable is covered with tiny roots.

Fibrous Roots

Have you ever brought home plants from a garden store to add to your garden? Have you ever looked at the roots of those plants? In each individual plant, you can see a good example of how roots grow. You might have noticed that roots grow away from the plant's stem, in search of water and minerals. In some plants, the roots grow and spread out over a very wide area to form what is called a fibrous root system. A plant with fibrous roots does not have one main root. Instead, its many roots are able to absorb water and minerals over a large area. Most of the roots are nearly the same size. They do not grow very deep into the soil, but they can be quite long. Grass and many trees have fibrous roots, as do most desert plants.

Taproots

Other plants have a root system that is made up of one very large, main root. This root is called a taproot. It does not spread over a large area the way a fibrous root does. Instead, it grows straight down into the soil. There it absorbs water and nutrients. As the taproot begins to store food for the plant, it grows thicker and wider. Beets, turnips, radishes, and carrots all have a taproot system.

Little hairs, which are actually roots, grow from the sides of the main taproot. Each hair absorbs water and minerals from the soil. They help the plant to grow by absorbing the necessary nutrients.

Radishes have a taproot system.

Plant Reproduction

Plants can be classified based on how they reproduce, or make new plants. Some plants, such as flowers and cone-bearing trees, reproduce by making seeds.

Most flowering plants have four parts. Petals are often pretty and brightly colored. They make the flower distinctive. They protect the parts of the flower that make seeds. They also attract living things, such as birds, butterflies, and bees, to the flower.

There are small, green leaves that lie below the petals. These leaves are **sepals.** Sepals keep the flower covered as it is growing in its bud. The sepals are pushed apart as the bud opens and the flower's petals spread.

In the center of each flower are small structures. These structures are part of the **pistil.** The smaller, stalklike structures that surround the pistil are the **stamens.** At the very ends of the stamens are the anthers. The anthers make little grains of pollen. A seed is made when the flower's egg combines with the sperm held by the pollen.

parts of a flower

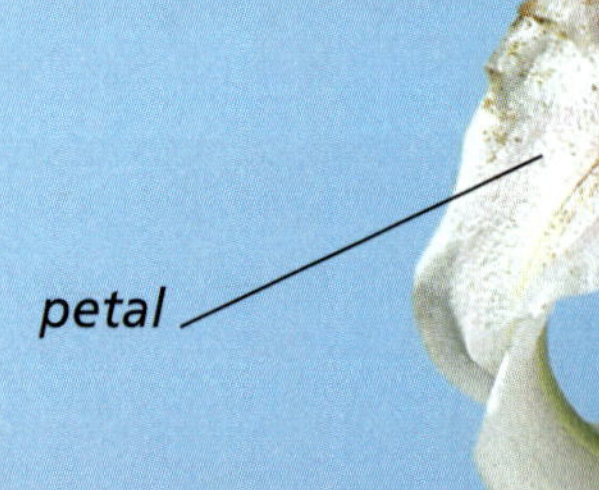

The four main parts of a flower's reproductive system are petals, sepals, stamens, and at least one pistil. Not all flowers have those four parts, however. The oak tree has separate female and male flowers. The female flowers have pistils and sepals. The male flowers have anthers and stamen. The sperm cells in the pollen of the anthers from the male flower combine with the eggs in the pistils of the female flower in order to make seeds.

Seeds can be made only when pollen moves from a stamen to a pistil. This is helped along in many different ways.

How Pollen Moves

Flowers make a liquid called nectar. It is sticky and sweet, and butterflies, birds, and bees are attracted to it. Many such animals fly from flower to flower looking for this sweet nectar. They are guided by the colors and smells of the flower. Pollen in the stamen rubs off onto an animal as it feeds on the nectar. Then, as the animal visits the next flower, that pollen might get rubbed onto a pistil. The way in which pollen moves from stamen to pistil is called pollination.

Pollination doesn't occur every time a bee visits a flower. But when it does happen, a pollen tube grows down through the pistil. The tube reaches the bottom part of the pistil, called the **ovary.** Egg cells live inside the ovary. Sperm cells that have been delivered to the pollen can then move down the pollen tube and reach the ovary. This is the process known as **fertilization.**

bee pollinating a dandelion

Fertilization

Once a flower is fertilized, it goes through many changes. The stamens and petals fall off, since they are no longer needed. The newly fertilized egg develops into a seed. The ovary grows and develops into a fruit, which protects the seed. Many of your favorite fruits are formed in this manner. Some are soft and fleshy, such as bananas, pears, and cherries. Others are more dry and hard. These include beans, peanuts, and acorns.

Animals do not pollinate all plants. Grass and trees often need help from wind in order to reproduce. Wind can move pollen from stamen to pistil, much as an animal does. Plants that depend on the wind don't have to attract animals, so they don't have to smell as sweet or have big flowers. Instead, these plants produce a lot of pollen. That makes it easy for the wind to do its job.

The petals of the rose attract bees for pollination.

After fertilization, the petals drop off.

Seeds develop inside the ovary.

The Life Cycle Of a Flowering Plant

bristlecone pine in California

A plant's life cycle is all the changes it goes through during its lifetime. How long a plant lives depends on the kind of plant it is. There is a bristlecone pine in California that is thought to be almost five thousand years old! Redwoods also live for a very long time—some for more than two thousand years. A plant such as a begonia or marigold normally lives for just a few months.

Conditions must be just right for a seed to begin growing. If it has the correct temperature and just the right amount of oxygen, sunlight, and water, it will swell and sprout through the seed coat. The food stored inside the seed feeds the young plant. Gravity helps push the little roots down into the soil. Its stem, which may appear weak, will look as if it's reaching for the Sun.

life cycle of a runner bean plant

The seed coat bursts open.

Soon the leaves will begin to grow, and photosynthesis will take place so the plant will have food. The plant will grow larger, and more leaves will form. It will grow into an adult plant and produce flowers and seeds. The plant's flowers will probably look very similar to the flowers its parents had. The plant may go on making flowers and seeds for many years. One day the plant will die, completing the life cycle.

Leaves appear, and photosynthesis can begin.

A root system develops, allowing the plant to absorb more nutrients from the soil.

How Seeds Move

Ask yourself what would happen if all the apples on an apple tree fell and landed in a heap below the tree. Some of the seeds would start to grow into new trees. But the parent tree's roots would be widely spread. They would be absorbing much of the water and minerals from the soil. The tree's shade would let only a little sunlight through to the new plants. So the apple seeds would not have enough living space, food, or water to grow. They would surely grow a lot better if some of the seeds moved, or were scattered, away from the tree. So plants have adaptations that help them scatter their seeds.

Apples collect at the base of an apple tree.

Animals Help

Many animals eat fruit. Fruit seeds can pass through an animal without breaking down. They end up within an animal's droppings on the ground, often far from the parent tree or plant.

The seeds of other fruits are covered with hooklike structures that can catch on the fur of animals or other objects. Animals carry these kinds of seeds, called burs, far away. When the hooked end breaks, the seed falls to wherever the animal happens to be.

Seeds can also grow far from a parent plant because some animals collect and then bury seeds and nuts for winter. Chipmunks, squirrels, kangaroo rats, and deer mice all do this. Many of the seeds are dug up and eaten, but others stay in the ground and grow after they have been buried.

squirrel

Wind and Water Help

Some plants have threads that act as parachutes. These so-called parachutes carry seeds with them if they are blown by wind or by a human. Dandelions are a common example of a parachutelike plant thread. Elm, birch, and oak trees are also pollinated with the wind's help. In parts of the United States, tumbleweeds are blown across the ground. As the plant rolls along, seeds fall off.

Other seeds and fruits float and move along waterways. Coconuts, which are the fruit of a palm tree, float from island to island. Wind and humans move the fruits from beach to beach, allowing new palm trees to grow. Yet many of these seeds do not become new plants.

Dandelion seeds are carried away by the wind.

Early Growth

Seeds fall to the ground all the time. But they may not begin to grow immediately. The amount of water, the oxygen level, and the temperature must be just right. When they are, the environment is perfect for growing a new plant.

Each seed contains a small plant. Food is stored in the seed to give it the energy it needs to begin to grow. But often the new environment is not right for the plant. If the seed cannot grow, it remains **dormant.** A seed can stay in this state of rest for days, weeks, seasons, or even years.

Spores

While many common plants and trees have flowers or cones that produce seeds, other plants produce spores in order to reproduce. Spores are very tiny, single cells. They contain very little food, so animals generally don't eat them. Spores can remain dormant for years and years. In order to grow, however, they must have wet ground.

Mosses and molds produce spores. They reproduce in two steps. The first step is when the plant produces a spore. That spore will not necessarily germinate. If it does germinate, however, it will become a plant with both male and female cells.

Spores are too tiny for you to see. However, they develop inside structures that can be seen on the underside of ferns.

The next step occurs when the female and male cells combine. The fertilized egg grows into a plant. This plant can then produce a new generation of spores.

Spore cases hold spores. When a spore case bursts open, the spores inside scatter into the air. Some spores drop to the ground near the parent plant. Wind and water carry others farther away. When the spore reaches its destination, it stays dormant until the moisture level and temperature are perfect. Then its life cycle continues.

spore case bursting open

New Plants from Plant Parts

Many plants grow from seeds. Others grow from spores. Still others grow from a plant's stems, roots, or leaves.

Plants that germinate in this way usually look exactly like the parent plant. For example, when you plant hyacinths, you do not begin with hyacinth seeds. You begin with bulbs, which are a type of underground stem. A bulb is made of many layers of thick leaves that store food. When the flower inside the bulb begins to grow, its leaves push out from the bulb. When those leaves push out of the soil, they become green. At that time they are able to make their own food through photosynthesis. Tulips, lilies, and some irises are other flowers that come from bulbs.

Some new plants begin by growing on the leaves of the parent plant. Some water lilies can sprout from the leaves of a parent plant.

A bulb has its own root system.

Some plants, such as strawberries and bamboo, have stems known as runners. They grow along the ground. The runners can develop roots that actually grow into the soil. Leaves will be able to grow from these roots.

If you cut a stem from a forsythia or an ivy plant and give it the right soil, temperature, and water, it will grow into a new plant. These stems are called sections, or cuttings. They can also be taken from a plant's leaves or roots.

Think about a peach tree grower who has some trees with strong roots that produce poor fruits. Other peach trees might have poor roots but produce excellent peaches. The grower can take branches from each tree and join them together. This is a complicated process called grafting. If conditions are right, it can produce beautiful, healthy plants.

Plants are more complicated than you might think. They can grow in many different ways. The next time you see a plant, think about where it comes from and what is going on underground!

parts of a strawberry plant

Glossary

chlorophyll a green pigment that is essential to photosynthesis

dormant temporarily inactive; in a state of suspended growth

fertilization the first step in biological reproduction, when a sperm and an egg join

ovary the part of a pistil that bears eggs

photosynthesis the process in which leaves that contain chlorophyll use sunlight to make food from carbon dioxide and water

pistil the portion of a flower where seeds develop

sepals the leaflike parts of a flower's base

stamens the pollen-producing portions of a flower